THE HOMESCHOOL
LETTERS

What we didn't know when we first started

Sarah Janisse Brown

& Fun-Schooling Moms

FunSchooling.com

ARE YOU GETTING STARTED WITH
HOMESCHOOLING?
Inspiration, Ideas & Helpful Tips!

NAME:_____

Art & Logic Activities to aWaken your Mind

Artwork and Logic Games

borrowed From "Lost & Found" Art & Logic Therapy – Brain Games

BY SARAH JANISSE BROWN

Letters From Homeschooling Mothers in the Facebook Group:

FUN-Schooling With Thinking Tree Books=

VISIT SARAH'S BLOG:

FUNSCHOOLINGWITHSARAH.COM

CREATE AN ENVIRONMENT OF NOURISHMENT AND PEACE

Do what it takes to create an environment where you and your children can thrive.

HOW TO USE THIS HANDBOOK:

Make your home peaceful by doing a few of the action steps above. Complete a page of logic, coloring and drawing. Read an inspiring letter from a homeschooling mom. Take notes or doodle a bit. When your children see you working on this book, they will be inspired by your example!

Dearest Mom,

If you are new to Homeschooling it can feel as if everything goes downhill fast. Kind of like making eggs, you want sunny side up but end up with scrabbled ones instead. It doesn't matter because the value and nutrition of the eggs stays the same. Your homeschooling will be what you need it to be in that season of your life.

Here is some advice I would like to share with you:
1. You are an Amazing Mom never forget that. When you are worried about your kids and what you are doing, that is your evidence.
2. Keep your Homeschool simple and uncomplicated.
3. If something is causing you or your kids' frustration during Education, DROP IT, kick it, Throw it out. If anything is causing you to want to pull your hair out it's not worth.
4. Your child can not fall behind.
Your child is an individual and your child will learn what he or she needs to when they are ready.
5. Do not let others dictate or bully you into doing something you feel would not work for your kids, trust your instincts they will never steer you wrong.
6. Take time for yourself. Even if it's just a 10min Coffee break. You need to take care of yourself to take care of everyone else. (We tend to forget that part)
7. Be open minded, you might be surprised at how much Education is hidden in real life duties.
8. Focus on your relationship with your kids. Play games have Fun, do not force Education, kids are naturally curious, use that to your advantage.

These are some of my top tips. Hope the help you on your New Adventure. Never be afraid to ask for help. We all need it sometimes.

Lots of Love,
Clerissa

My dearest Mom,

You are about to embark on the most rewarding journey of your child's life. In the years to come you will witness countless moments that so many parents miss out on. You will see your child discover passions and develop new skills. You have made the choice to be your child's biggest influence. With this choice will come many tears of joy and frustration. You may have days you question the choice you made. You likely will encounter people that don't support you. All of this is okay you will find your strength. Never forget the reason you started your journey. Your path may change daily but the reason you started can be your anchor. Always remember they are children first and students second. Sometime everyone just needs a long break and that's okay also.

Molly DeJourdan

NOTES, DOODLES, IDEAS AND TASKS:

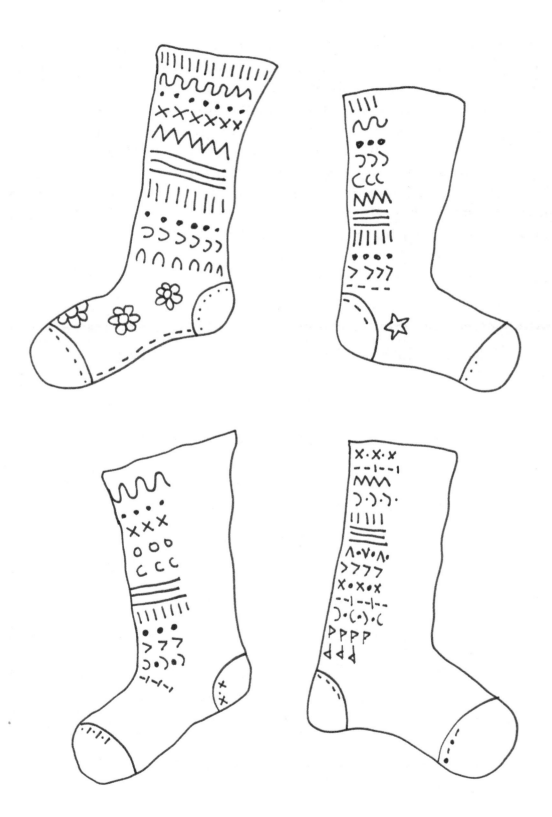

Dear new homeschooling mama,

I'm writing this to you, as I sit here, wearing a "Viking" helmet made of tinfoil (nose piece included), courtesy of my 9-year-old. Can I offer you some advice? Stop what you're doing. Stop riding the homeschool Google bus. Stop asking Facebook what to do. Stop scrolling Instagram homeschool pages. You'll soon find out that the world of sepia-toned homeschool flat lays only belongs on Instagram, not real life with real messy kids.

Take a deep breath. Get down on your knees and really look at your children. Give them a big bear hug. Look into their eyes and know that they are worth the journey. Cuddle up, read some good books, play in nature, enjoy the company of your kids, and relax knowing that you've got what it takes. Then, trust that your kids are going to have what it takes to learn what they need to, when they need to, how they need to. Embrace this adventure.

• Also, word of warning, be ready to spend your life savings on tinfoil... always add tinfoil.
Cheering for you,

Jessie

NOTES, DOODLES, IDEAS AND TASKS:

ADD WORDS, DOODLES AND COLOR.

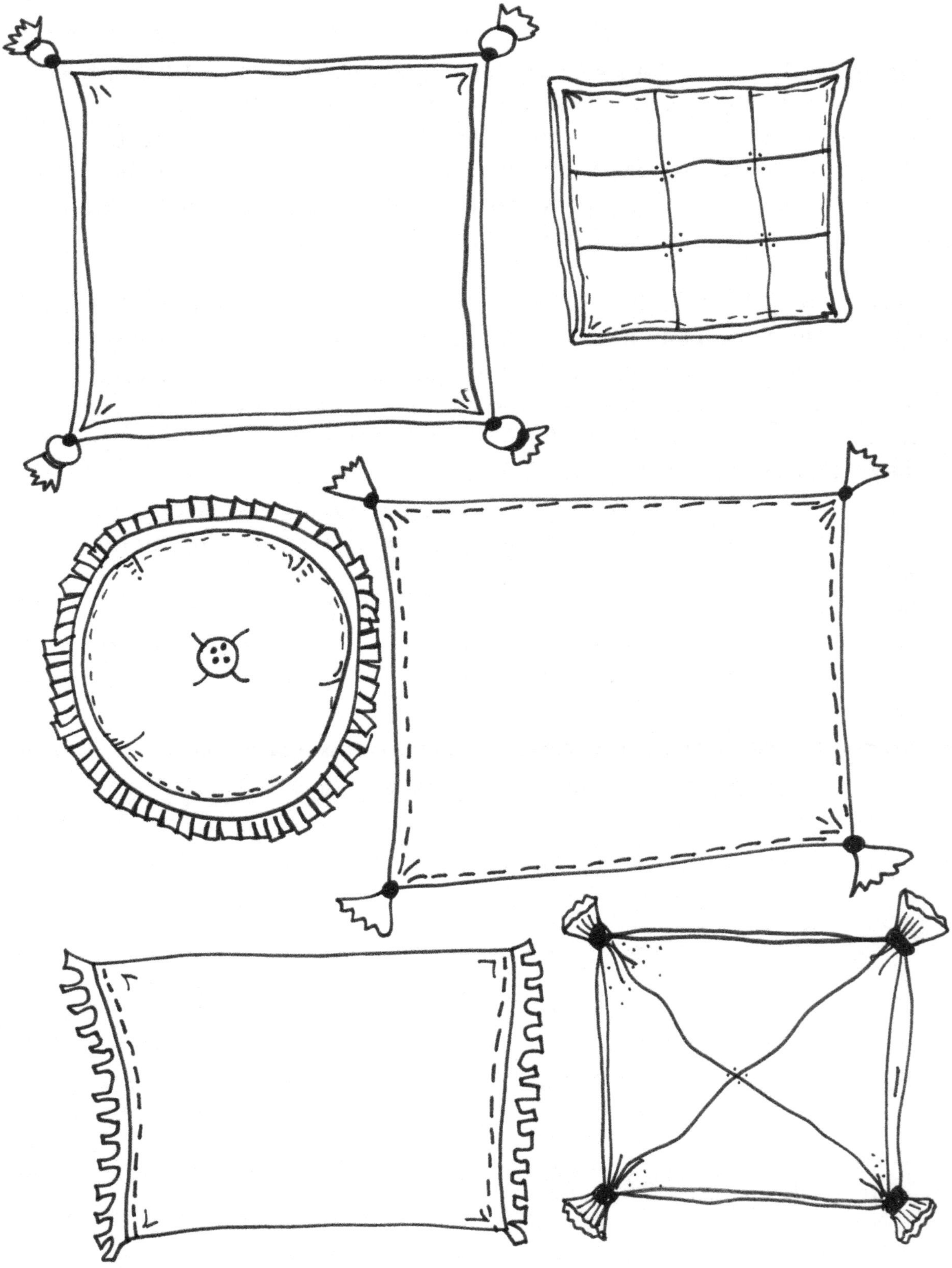

To the mama asking, "How do I do it?",

Turn away from those who mock you and tell you that you can't. Face those who want to support you and tell you that you can. Don't put your time into trying to impress those who are watching, but support and impress your own kids. Make sure you trust your instincts and remember that no single purchase will make your homeschool a success.

Homeschooling is more than a curriculum; it is a lifestyle that you will create and mold into your ideal environment.

Let go of your expectations and let your children bloom into the people they were meant to be. They may not grow up to be a doctor or lawyer, but they can grow up to be happy doing something they truly love. Don't be afraid to go against the grain and teach them the morals and values you feel are the most important. There is no need to fit into the world outside your home. Teach your littles the value of integrity and honesty so they can be respected when they go out into the world.
Children are capable of learning and discussing big ideas so don't shy away from good conversations. And when life gets hard don't be afraid to take a break from your years plan. Life is messy, things won't always go as planned, and you won't screw up your kids. Why? Because you care.

Most importantly read lots of books, play hard, listen to music, play games, make art, and grow bonds. Enjoy the time you have with your children; you have given yourself a precious gift- time.

Christine Owens

NOTES, DOODLES, IDEAS AND TASKS:

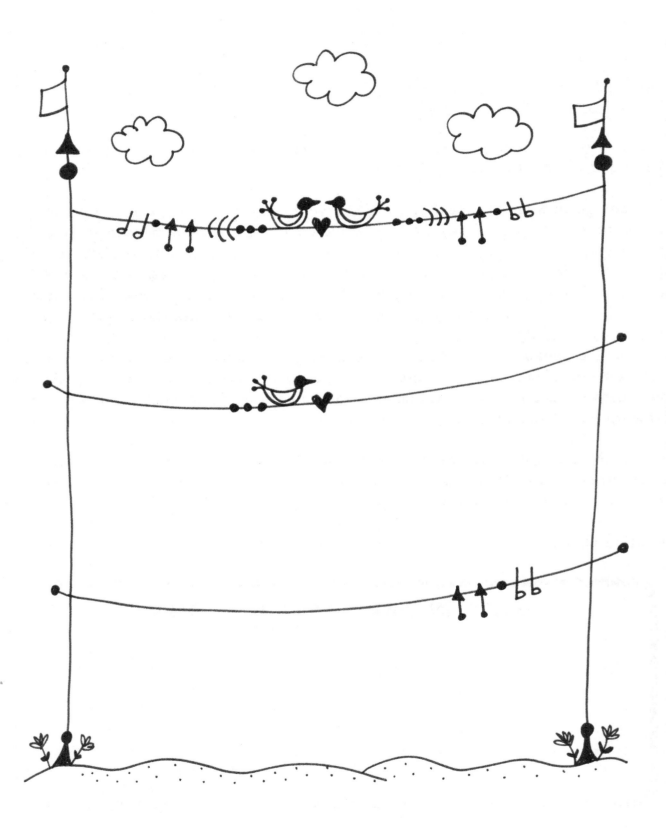

Dear Momma,

Homeschooling is such a blessing. You will create so many memories with your little one. Please do not think it'll be picture perfect like they make it seem in movies. You will have days that you struggle to get anything done. You will have people in your ear making you question your decision. It's okay. Do not let people get to you.

You got this! Just keep in mind you are doing what is best for your family. You are doing amazing!

Dallas Brothers

NOTES, DOODLES, IDEAS AND TASKS:

Dear homeschool mama,

As were out soaking in the sunshine this morning, I would love to challenge you. I want to challenge you to read the books and smell them too, to make a mess of your kitchen with late breakfast, and science projects. I challenge you to do the bookwork, but when the days grow stale, shut them, and go outside, and run, find the bugs and the birds, and feel the earth under your feet. Show your babies how to live, how to love, how to read and write, how to do the math, the history facts but most of all teach them life. Life isn't perfect and clear cut, it's messy, and loud, and frustrating and beautiful, it hurts and its breath taking. Live mamas and teach.

Melissa Gemoules

NOTES, DOODLES, IDEAS AND TASKS:

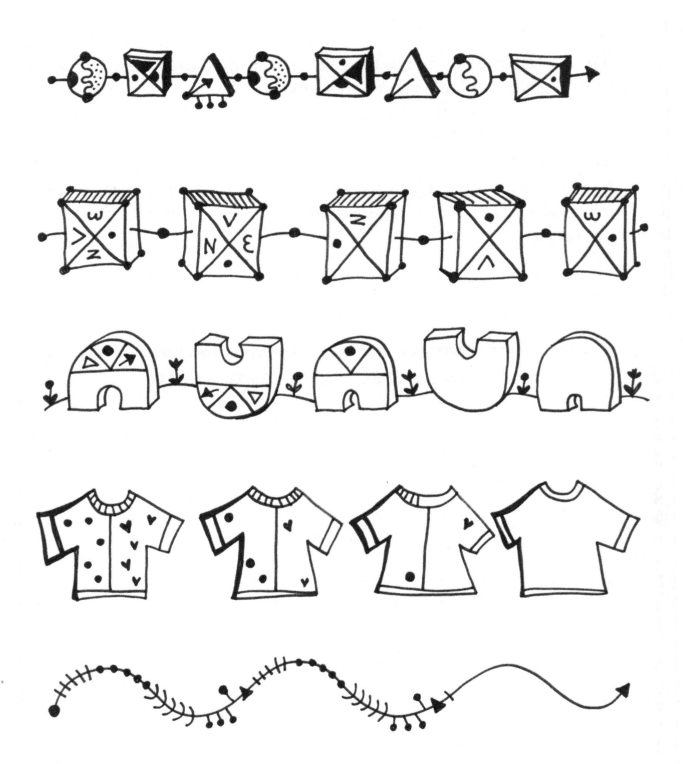

Dear new homeschool mom,

I want to congratulate you for choosing to enter the world of homeschooling. Please don't feel overwhelmed. Take everything you know about your past and create a new way of doing things when it comes to educating your children. Observe and listen to your child. It will be a journey of discovery. We learn in different ways, and you will be able to find out your child's learning style. Enjoy this new adventure. I want to remind you that you will not be alone. First, God will help you and those people that you trust will become wonderful blessings in your life. There are homeschool communities everywhere. Plug in with local groups. Join online homeschool groups. You can ask any question in those groups. You will find people that love to help by answering your questions. Find local church or community programs that match your kids' interest like sports, performing arts, etc. My children always loved being a part of these places. Homeschooling is also a time to work on character. There are so many ways to do it. God will be your guide and strength.

Sincerely, Diana L (homeschool mom for 17 years)

NOTES, DOODLES, IDEAS AND TASKS:

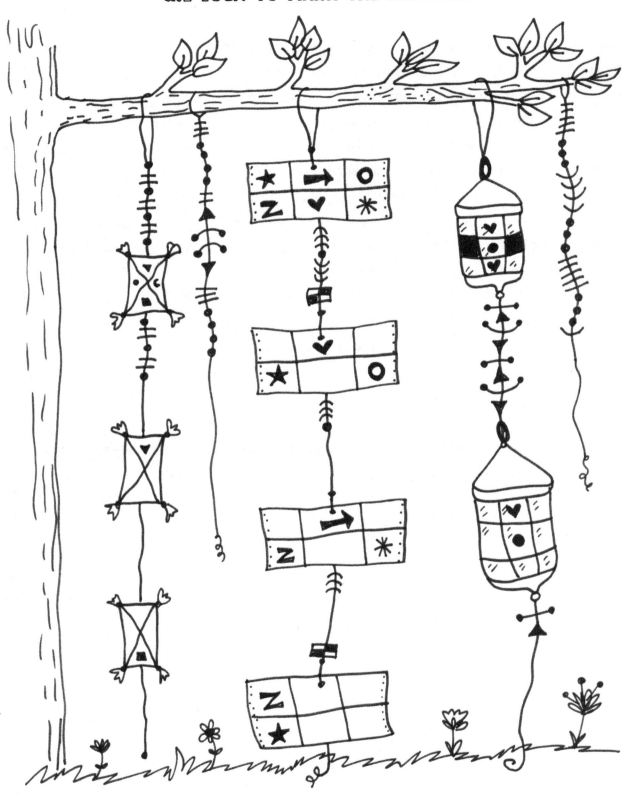

Dear new homeschool mom,

     Homeschooling is an exciting and fun adventure you and your child(ren) will take together. Take time to embrace it and be willing to follow their lead. The biggest warning I give to you is homeschooling is not school at home. You do not have to reproduce the setting or activities of what is done in a classroom. With homeschooling the world you live in is your classroom and the children will explore it and create things to make it better. We as mamas are to encourage this behavior and try to open our minds to the child's viewpoint. We are to supply them with resources and opportunities the engage with the world around them and encourage the designs they have for life. The kitchen is one of the best places for Reading, Math, and Science to occur. Take what you have use it. Outside is a great place for lots of learning. Also, remember being active and engaged often actually produces more learning than sitting in a desk. (My oldest learned to read by walking around the table.)
Have fun and enjoy life while learning with your child(ren).

Sarabeth Peavey

NOTES, DOODLES, IDEAS AND TASKS:

ADD WORDS, DOODLES AND COLOR.

Dear Mom (Dad, Grandparent),

Thank you for making our next generation your priority. You are about to venture out on a journey that, like all important things, will involve some sacrifice but will pay a thousand-fold in blessings. Everyone's journey is different, but here are a few things I've learned in 7 years of public-school teaching and 15 at home.

Every child is unique. Kids in traditional schools must move forward as a group due to the constraints of the environment, but even the best schools and classrooms don't suit the needs of everyone all the time. So, if your kiddo loves science, give them lots of it. God made them for a purpose, and He knows what He is doing! If they struggle to write, help them learn but don't feel like you or they are failing if they don't write like your neighbor's kid. Be mom first. Put the relationship first, the person they were made to be first, and it will all fall in place.

Find community, mama. It may take lots of play dates, different co-ops, activities, and trying different things but find your people, your tribe, and then be real with them and embrace them. It will help you and your child immensely.

Finally, have fun. The very best days will be watching your child light up and grow while they learn things you never knew and teach them to you. Snuggle them on the couch and read. Go outside and explore the wonders of creation. Do the things they cannot do in a desk with 25 other kids and watch them thrive. Then, take a nap. You may need it!

Chris DeWitt

NOTES, DOODLES, IDEAS AND TASKS:

Dear homeschooling mama,

I know right now you are feeling overwhelmed. You want only the best for your child. I'm here to reassure you that you are not alone. My advice to you would be to find a support system. While a spouse is your number one supporter, I find talking with other moms, especially experienced ones, to be a tremendous value. Find a likeminded homeschool group either online or ask your local librarian if she/he knows of any groups. Always remember why you pursued the home-schooling route. Always keep the end goal in mind. There isn't anyone who loves your child more than you do! I wish you only the best on your journey!

Sincerely,
Kelly Levesque, a fellow homeschooling mama

NOTES, DOODLES, IDEAS AND TASKS:

Dear new homeschooling mom,

It's ok if you feel it in your heart that this is right for you. Meet some fellow homeschoolers or join some Facebook groups for support. Think about what your true reason for wanting to homeschool is and don't lose sight of that reason. It's ok to decide to try a year as a trial run to discover how much you love it.

There will be hard days, some days you might yell or cry and it's ok! If one same thing is causing hard days repeatedly, please have the courage to stop it and change it. Recognize what works for you and your family. Learn what type of learner your kid is (or kids) and what their interests are. Find what gives them joy and prepares them for life! Most importantly remember, you're doing a great job and it will all be ok.

Yours truly,
Janie Hamilton, 6 years homeschool mama

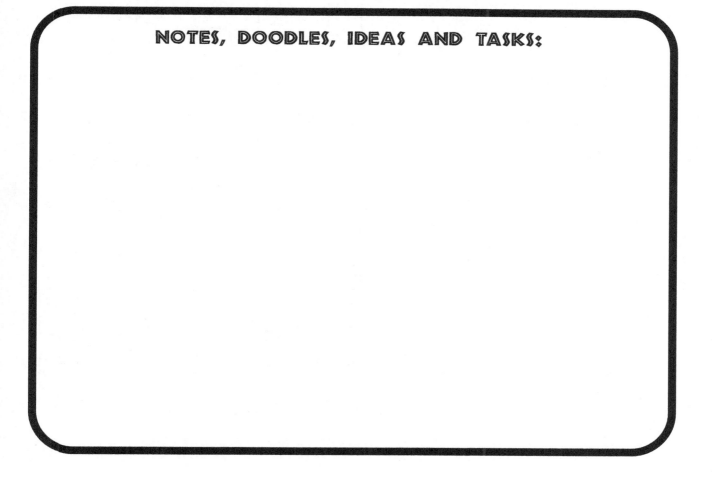

NOTES, DOODLES, IDEAS AND TASKS:

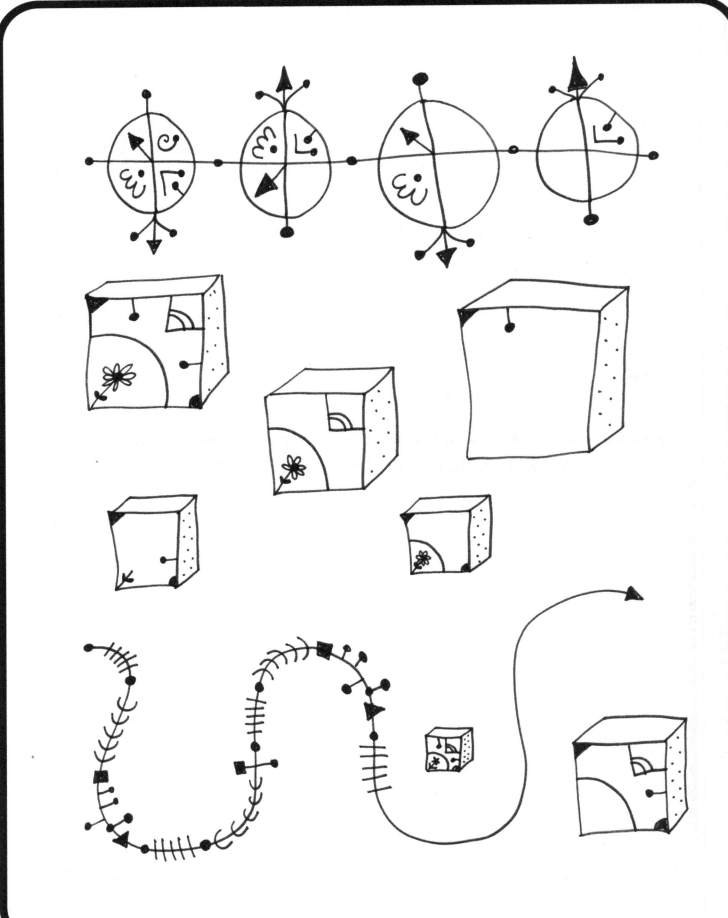

Dearest homeschooling hero,

Yes, hero! First, breathe- everything will be okay. You've made a brave, brave decision. I know your mind is probably being pulled in all directions. Mine was too. I kept questioning my capabilities. Am I smart enough? Am I organized enough? Am I patient enough? Will I fail my children? As valid as these fears are, remember- your child/children is/are capable. More than capable! They are smart, brave, and resilient! They couldn't have gotten that way without amazing, loving, capable parents. You are more than enough!

The best advice I can give is to first, investigate de-schooling. You and (possibly) your kiddo(s) must unlearn what you think school looks like. Set out some FUN educational games, workbooks, puzzles, arts and crafts, toys, etc. and watch them. See how much they learn and grow despite not having structured learning and guidance. You can observe and learn their own individual styles through unstructured schooling. School can be baking cookies, or a trip to the library. It can be taking a walk and observing the world around you or sitting together doing a workbook. It can be whatever you want!

Second, you will most likely go through a lot of different curricula. It will change and grow with your child(ren) as they change and grow and learn and re-learn what works best for them. The library is a wonderful free resource for that trial and error, or you could even see if you can find other local homeschool families and see if you can borrow their curriculum. This brings me to the dreaded comment you'll never stop hearing. "What about socialization?!" First let me say, my kids socialize tenfold more now that we homeschool. We meet with other homeschool families at least once a week and do many extracurricular things. For example, they're currently taking a homeschool karate class, homeschool horseback riding, and a homeschool archery class! We are blessed to live in a time of technology and social media. I'm sure if you hop on Facebook, you will find local homeschool families, groups, and meet ups. You can also check your local libraries, churches, nature centers, and museums for homeschooling activities. It may take a little while, but you will find your people, and so will your kiddo(s).

This will be the most rewarding and, I can't lie- challenging experience. The joy of seeing your child thrive and love learning (on most days...I mean they are children) is immeasurable. We only get 18 beautiful years with our sweet babes. What a tremendous blessing to have so many days, hours, and minutes to help shape them into kind, loving, amazing human beings.

Congratulations on your decision, and remember to enjoy the journey because that's where the joy is, eh?

Love,
A fellow "crazy" homeschooling Mama

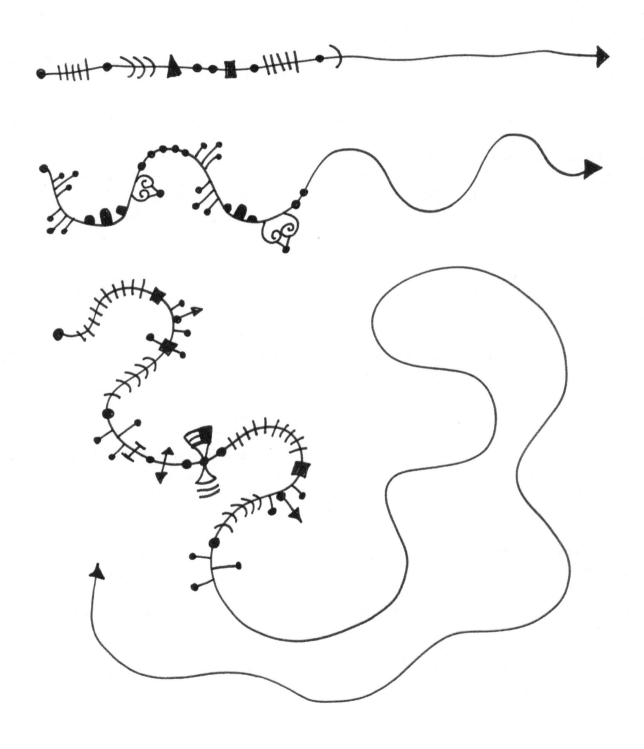

Hey there Mumma,

You've got this! I know it most likely feels really overwhelming, but I applaud your bravery. This is one of the hardest, but most rewarding choices you will ever make. I want you to know that your journey is not going to look like anyone else's. Your family is as unique as each of our fingerprints are. What works for another family might not work for you. That's ok. Take each moment at a time, knowing that you know your children better than anyone else. You love them, and because of that you will not fail them. Don't be scared to keep it simple, and when all else fails, go back to the basics.

Dream! Chase those interests! Read! Learning happens through every moment. Allow your children to live wildly, creatively and in a way that inspires them to be who they were born to be.

Jeanne Burne

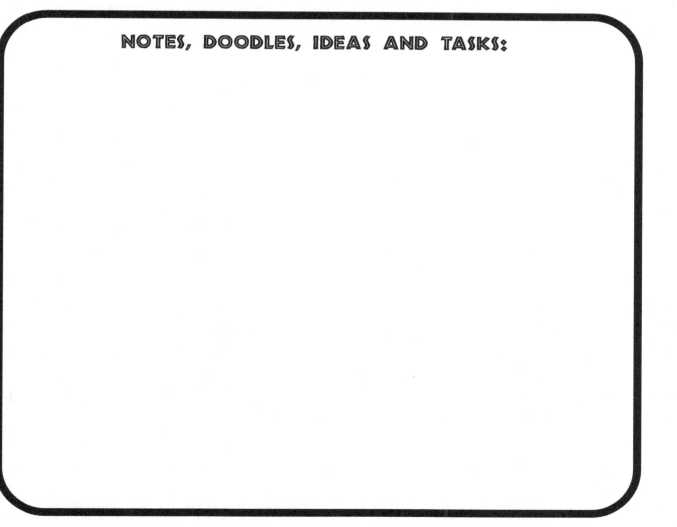

NOTES, DOODLES, IDEAS AND TASKS:

Hey Mama,

I believe when I was in school homeschool wasn't really talked about. It was what the "weird" kids did. Now, I know that's the furthest from the truth. I truly believe homeschool allows kids to be who God called them to be. Homeschooling will allow you as a parent to learn & grow with your child. Also, homeschooling allows you to teach your kids how you want and what you want. I love teaching my children about things they are passionate about. Don't doubt yourself but trust the process. Trust yourself and your children. Trust the Lord gave you the tools you need to thrive. Most importantly, use this as a time to bond and connect with your children. One day, we will look back and thank God we were the "weird ones".

Love,
Noel, child of God

NOTES, DOODLES, IDEAS AND TASKS:

Dear Momma,

You've got this. You have been chosen to educate your child(ren) at home, and you've got this. Simply follow your heart in what and how you lead your child to learning and know that there is never a "perfect" day. Nope. Not a one. But there WILL be many perfect moments. Cherish them all. And always keep a healthy sense of humor because you're going to need it!

Yep. You've got this. And the icing on the cake? You are not alone in this big, beautiful homeschool world. Now, go have some fun.

Wholeheartedly,
Ruby Resch

NOTES, DOODLES, IDEAS AND TASKS:

Hey Momma,

     I know in the beginning it seems crazy, like a big scramble for supplies and curriculum and there are so many choices and so much to do and are you ever going to get everything done? Stop. Breathe. You're okay. The kids are going to be okay. You aren't competing with anybody. You don't have to focus on grades and standards – you are preparing your child for a life and a career outside your home, as the person they were meant to be and not what society or the government wants to mold them into. Your kids will gain more from being home with you – even if you teach them nothing on your own and let them take the entire lead – than they ever would have in a public school. You don't have to be perfect – nobody is. There are going to be gaps – public school also has gaps. Just relax. They're going to be prepared and you are all going to have wonderful memories of all the days spent together. The scariness will go away. Just enjoy everything else.

With love,
Ashley "Formerly Frazzled" Bedford

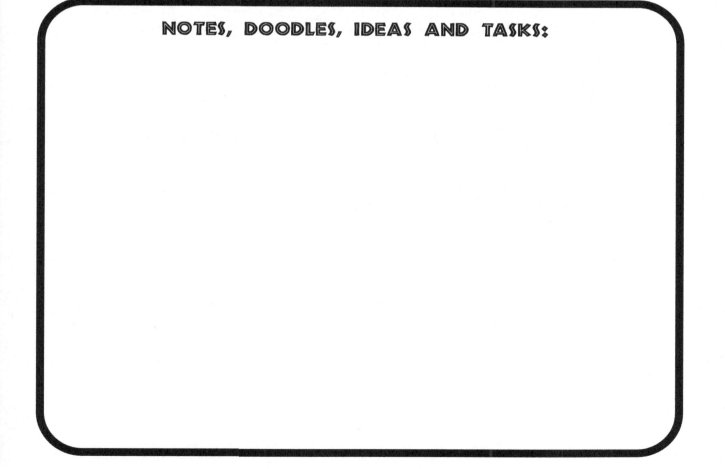

NOTES, DOODLES, IDEAS AND TASKS:

Dear Mom,

You can do this! If something doesn't work that doesn't mean you failed, or that your child failed. It means you're learning how your child learns and you can try something new. It means you can reassure your child that you will figure it out together. If something works, then celebrate! Things that work might not make "sense". School in your underwear, school outside, school on Saturday. Who cares? Listen to your child. Do what you believe to be right and good and true. If others have something to say about it, then fine. Listen for the wisdom and discard the negativity. Be willing to be wrong and learn from your mistakes and teach your child to do the same. Enjoy the extra time you have with them and apologize when you're too hard on them, because it will happen! Don't be afraid to ask for help, and remember, you know your child better than anyone, so you can do this.

Love, Susanna Tirinato

NOTES, DOODLES, IDEAS AND TASKS:

Dear homeschool mom/dad,

I'm writing you this letter to tell you a truth you may not know. A truth you may not even believe. You are enough. Did you hear me? YOU, you are enough. Not just in the good times, but all the time. You're enough if your experience looks different. when you feel unappreciated, burned out, powerless, unsure, doubted, or totally alone (even in a crowded room). You're enough if you lose your temper, decide to keep things simple, and even when you need to ask for help. Are you still listening?

No one loves your family deeper, nor fights harder, nor knows them better than you. Some days, this incredible journey is a breeze. Other days, you need reminding.

So, I tell you again, my sister/brother, my friend, my partner; dare I say...myself, without hesitation, YOU ARE ENOUGH.

With love and deep admiration,
R.P.

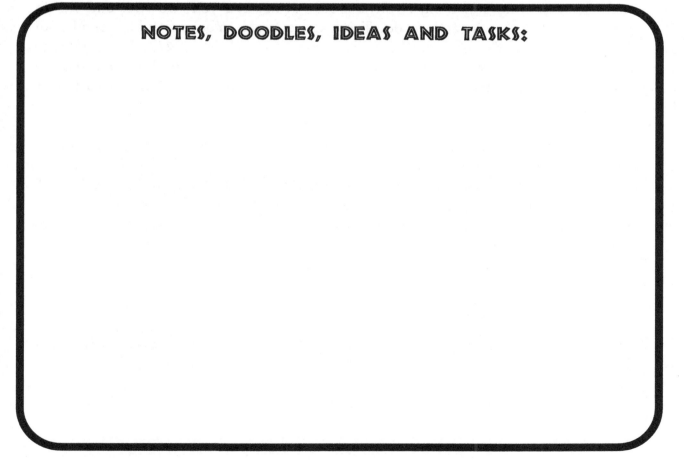

NOTES, DOODLES, IDEAS AND TASKS:

To the mom of young children who is just beginning this journey,

Seek delight. Find joy. Be present for the present, the gift of this moment. It's a once in a lifetime opportunity. Enjoy it. Rest in it. This is a mindset thing. Until you do the hard work of recognizing and then changing your own thoughts about living, loving, and learning, you will struggle with homeschooling.

Homeschooling can feel like a cage or a heavy weight. It can be scary and let's face it, mothering can bring out the worst in us. We yell, we fail, and we do the opposite of what we intend to do. There is no break. You can't just send your kids off to school for the day and rest. No, they are with you 24/7. It's a marathon and it's exhausting. There is always more to do in a day than can be done and it's easy to let your own self-care slip. Yet, taking care of yourself is a key to learning how to take care of your kids.

You are the greatest example. You are the lead learner. Do you know what nourishes you? What do you enjoy doing? Do you take time to do it? Are you living a high-quality life, the kind of life that you want your kids to grow up and live? Do you like yourself? Do you like learning? Do you like your life? Do you like your kids? Do your kids know that you like them? They need to know that you delight in them. They need to know that they are your treasure, and you delight to invest your life in them. This work is a joy and not a burden. It's a mindset thing. Discover the thoughts that are killing your joy and replace them with thoughts that fill you with joy.

To do this, I must get away for a few minutes. I need a few minutes to calm down, to pray and to write. I ask God for wisdom, and He gives it. In the middle of my crazy chaos, I must pull myself out of it, knowing that my attitude, my thoughts, my words, and my actions are creating more problems than I am solving. I sit down on my bed, and I cry.

I ask my questions: "Why am I so triggered by this?" "Why is it so hard for me to _____?" I journal and I seek answers. I have mantras I say to myself every day, several times a day, and they help me to change my thoughts, my attitudes, my words, and my actions. Here are some of mine.

When I am feeling frustrated or overwhelmed by the messes: "I create beauty everywhere I go."
When academic pressures and my expectations for our homeschool are making us miserable: "Restful relationship." My goal, my trump card. This phrase puts every other expectation in perspective. When I don't like my reality and want to escape from it in one way or another: "Be present for the present, the gift of this moment." (Really, this is practicing gratitude in the mind.)
When I am tired and depleted: "It's okay to rest." "Rest is best."

When I am sad, depressed, grieving hard losses, and hiding in my cave God whispers to my heart, "It's okay to cry. I see you. I love you." I imagine Him holding me and I let myself feel it all. I have learned that you can't get through the pain to joy on the other side by pretending that the pain isn't there. The wounds fester and they need to heal. Healing takes time.

Through all of this, I am learning and growing, and I am modeling to my children what it means to learn and to grow. I want them to be healthy and joyful, kind and loving. That means that I need to be that kind of person myself and live that kind of life. These are the most important things, more important than academics and achievements.
Also, with young children, just enjoy your time with them. Let them play. Inspire their play with something that inspires you. Share your own joy in learning something new. Read together. Rest together. Work together. Invite them to join you in your work. When you see that they are interested in something, provide a feast of learning opportunities, creating a rich and diverse learning environment. Some young children are much more interested in learning to read than others. It's okay. The same goes for math. Most kids enjoy listening to stories, but my boys always wriggled lots and lots. They wanted to be laying on the floor, playing with toys or Legos while I read to them and that was okay with me. I make my "one-on-one" time with my little kids, quality time together, whether we are just snuggling and playing or singing phonics songs and practicing handwriting or math calculations.

The key to your children learning anything is their own desire to learn it. If the desire is not there and you push them anyway, it will just be frustrating for both of you and it probably won't work very well. I have learned this the hard way with my dyslexic children. Patience is key. Trust your kids and refuse to let fear of _____ (them never learning to read) undermine your time with them. Believe the best and let time do the rest. I'm not saying be lazy and do nothing about your kids' learning struggles. I'm just saying that acting in fear always does more damage to relationships than it is worth, even when it is used to motivate us through obstacles. There is a better way. Trust the process. Remember, this is a long journey, and you are in it for the long haul.

Lots of love,
Rose Kolterman, a homeschooling mom of seven delightful children.

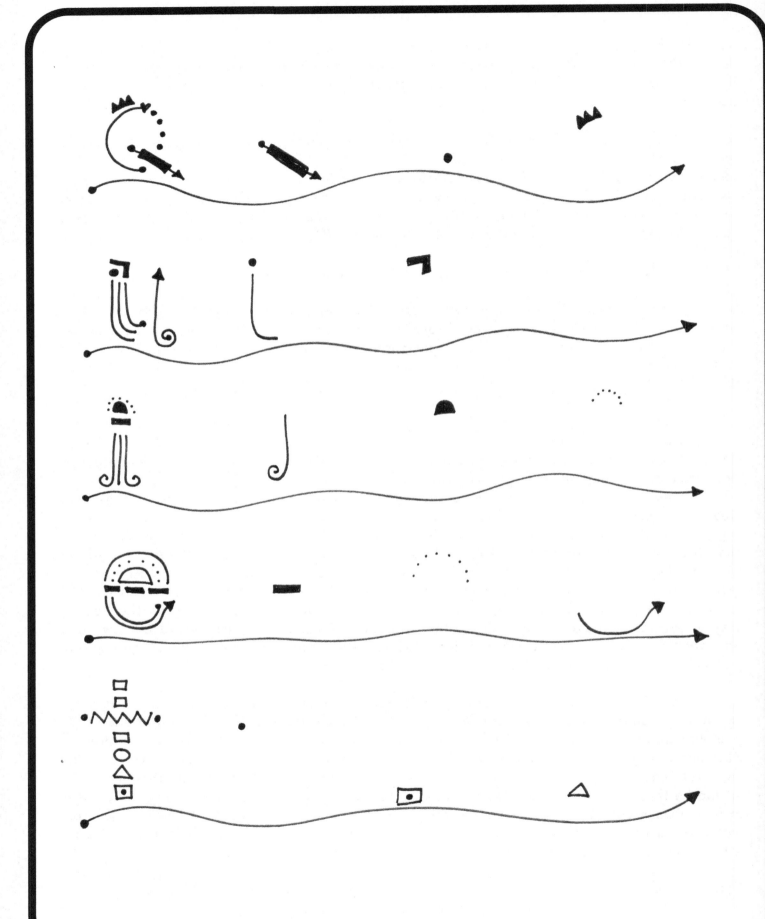

Homeschooling mom,

You made the choice to homeschool- that's huge! First step, done. You did it!
Next step, just show up. Ask your kids to "just show up". We all have dreams and visions for what we want homeschooling to look like, but through all those well laid plans, hold tight to why you are homeschooling, not what you are homeschooling. Take lots of breaks, escape to the bathroom, look yourself in that mirror and smile. Remind yourself that YOU can absolutely do this.

Allie Marie

NOTES, DOODLES, IDEAS AND TASKS:

Dear new homeschool mom,

You have taken such a huge step and I know it feels daunting. Just take a step back and breath. We have all been where you are now. We have all felt like we have been pushed into the deep end without a safety rope. It will be okay. It is going to take a few months for yourself, and your children to find your footing. When you do you will not only swim, but you will also soar! The possibilities are endless! Some days you will be investing bugs in the garden and other days be lost in a book. When the days are tough, remember why you are doing this, breath, and bake cookies. You are enough, and remember to give yourself, and your children, grace.

Good luck on your new journey.

Love from Carmen

NOTES, DOODLES, IDEAS AND TASKS:

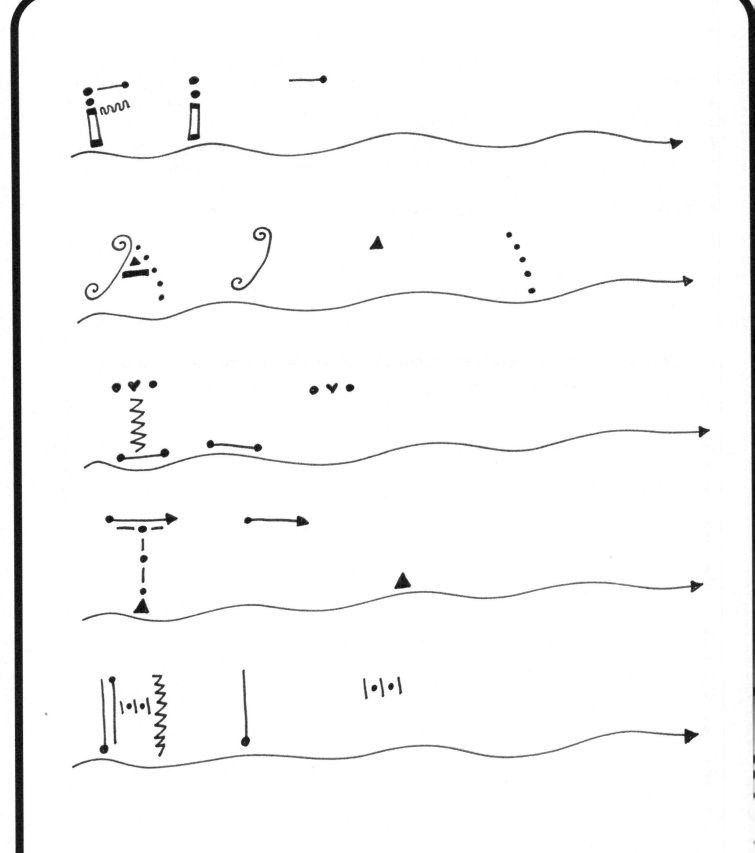

Mom,

I know you're scared, excited, curious, anxious, overwhelmed! The what if's can be all-consuming, mixed with the curriculum choices, the teaching styles, the learning styles, "I can do this," "I can't do this.", "How does anyone do this?!"

Stop! Breathe. You had it right the first time. You can do this! You're not alone! Even if you are, you still have that sweet child of yours and all your love to propel you in this journey. Your child wants to learn, and you want so much for your child. How will you do it all? You won't. Your child will help you by letting you know what they want to learn, you will prioritize the necessities and most important things. You will teach your child through your own example that learning is a fun and continuous process even into adulthood. You'll make mistakes, you'll make amends, and you'll grow along the way.

This is a journey traveled a moment at a time. Grab some tea, grab an idea, grab your child's hand, and enjoy the scenery along the way. You've got this!

Keep the love in everything,
Lynnea

NOTES, DOODLES, IDEAS AND TASKS:

Dear new homeschooling mama,

Your gut led you to this decision, trust it! Your brain did all the research, trust it! Your heart knows what your kids need, trust it! You will have days when it's hard; accept those days: close the books, snuggle up, eat snacks, and try tomorrow! You will have days when it's great; lean in and let the kids do the projects and make the mess!

Always remember, your relationship with your kids is more important than any learning. They will remember how they felt about learning way more than what they learned.

Best of luck!
Alex Romano

NOTES, DOODLES, IDEAS AND TASKS:

Dear fellow homeschooler,

Welcome to the club! Not every day is going to be sunshine and rainbows. There will be tears (from the kids & from you). Others may judge your decisions, but please know that you are making a difference and that your decision to home-school is good and valid. Don't try to recreate a classroom setting. Involve your child(ren) in selecting subjects of interest to them. Don't stick with something that isn't working. Get outside! Remember that learning comes in all shapes and forms. Make learning fun! But most importantly, take a deep breath and relax. You don't have to have everything figured out on day one. Ask for help, get involved in online and/or in person homeschool groups, and try new things whenever possible. Find your community and embrace this amazing way of educating your child(ren).

Lots of Love,
Laine

NOTES, DOODLES, IDEAS AND TASKS:

Dear Mama,

Take a deep breath and settle down on the couch with your kiddos and a good book.
Literally, that's the first step. Next, realize you can't do this homeschool journey on your own. God **HAS** equipped you for it, with His help. Lean into Him. Your child is uniquely crafted with personalized details that don't always conform to "standards", and that's okay. It's more than okay. It's amazing!
Teach your child how to learn. Teach them to teach themselves. Show them learning is fun and enjoyable. Show them it's okay to fall, to not be perfect, to make mistake- just get back up.
You, mama, are perfectly equipped for this monumental task. You got this.

Whitney B.

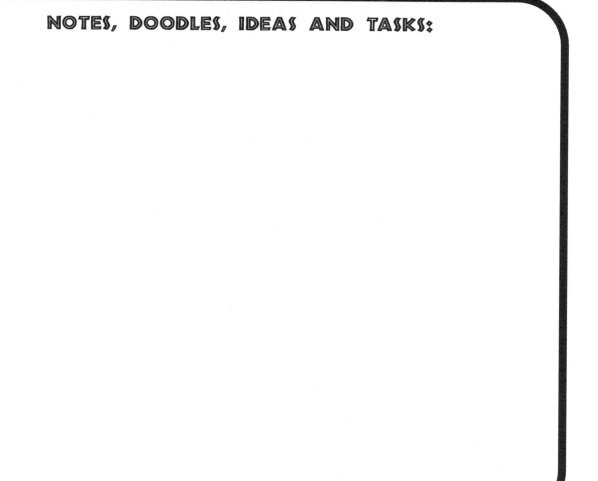

NOTES, DOODLES, IDEAS AND TASKS:

Yay Mama,

You did it! You made a life-changing decision and took on the brave new world of homeschooling. This is such an exciting and terrifying time. You may be questioning if you made the right decision. You may be hearing a lot of external noise from family, friends, all the new homeschool groups you've joined, etc. It is so easy to fall into the comparison trap and start filtering everything you do (or don't do) through someone else's idea of perfect. Homeschooling is not a one-size-fits-all endeavor. Your homeschool is as beautifully unique as your children and yourself! Do not spend your time trying to fit your homeschool into someone else's box of perfection. Embrace all the wonderful gifts and passions you and your children have! You were called to homeschool for a reason, and you have been equipped with everything you need to give your children the absolute best education and life possible. Enjoy every moment of this amazing journey!

May you be abundantly blessed,
MaKenzie Alberdi

NOTES, DOODLES, IDEAS AND TASKS:

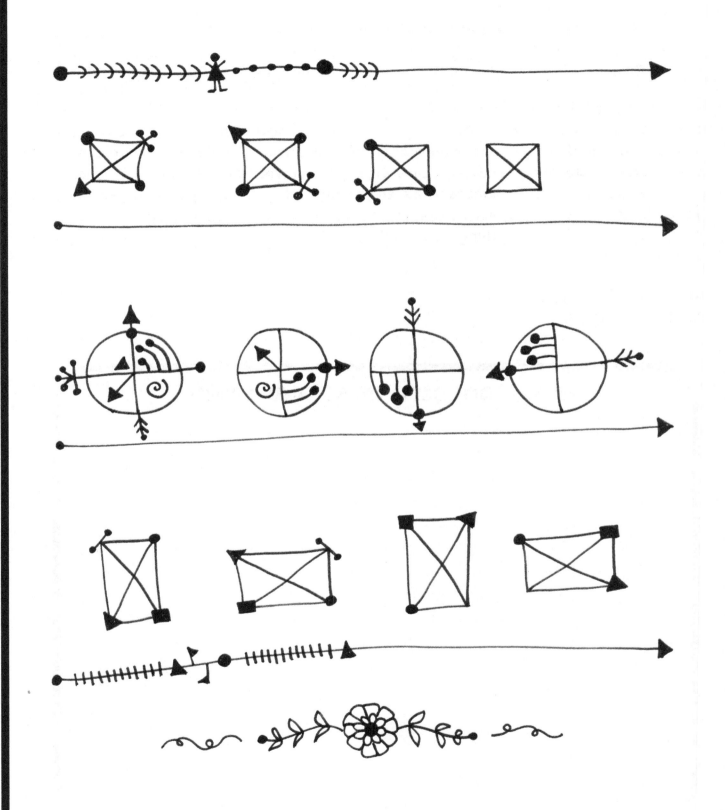

Dear Mama,

Congratulations on your new journey! What an exciting time for you and your family! I'm sure you have tons of plans and maybe are overwhelmed with options. It's okay- just take it slowly. You will get tons of advice about how kids learn and letting littles play instead of doing book work. Some is right for your family, but some is not, and some you might not be ready to hear yet on this point of your journey. You must decide what is right for your family in each stage, and while it's nice to get advice, no one knows what will really work for your kiddos and you. You don't have to know it all or figure it all out to be making beautiful memories and learning together.

The hardest advice for me was when moms told me not to worry or not to stress. Looking back, I wish I could have relaxed and enjoyed the process more (I know my kids were enjoying homeschooling!), but that's the phase I was in. You do have this mama!! It's okay to not know it all now. You won't ever have it totally figured out and will learn to be okay with that. And it's okay if not having it totally figured out stresses you out now too. It really is just a season. And everything is going to be okay- all this effort you are putting in now is totally worth it. I believe in you!

Brittany, 7 years and 5 kids into this homeschooling life

NOTES, DOODLES, IDEAS AND TASKS:

To the parent who chose to walk alongside their child(ren) on this unknown path,

The path is unknown to most and chosen by few but is so much more scenic and rewarding than any other. There will come days when you want to turn back, when you feel that the road is getting tough, but the toughest routes often lead to the best undiscovered treasures. There will be people who tell you to steer clear of what lies ahead, but these people only do so because they themselves are too afraid to venture out and take the risk of being free. Do not become discouraged. Do not give up. When the road gets long and hard, look at who you are traveling with, look at how you all have grown, look at what you have learned along the way, and go on to find those amazing things and places along the way.
Take time to admire and celebrate the small things that other parents never get to experience. Celebrate the time your child finally uses more than one color to color their pictures. Celebrate the time your child counts in 3's. Celebrate your child reading their 1st, 2nd and even 10th book. Celebrate life, your family, your journey.

Best of luck and remember to sometimes leave the paved road behind and look for hidden treasure along the way.

Love, Mamma Elaine O.

NOTES, DOODLES, IDEAS AND TASKS:

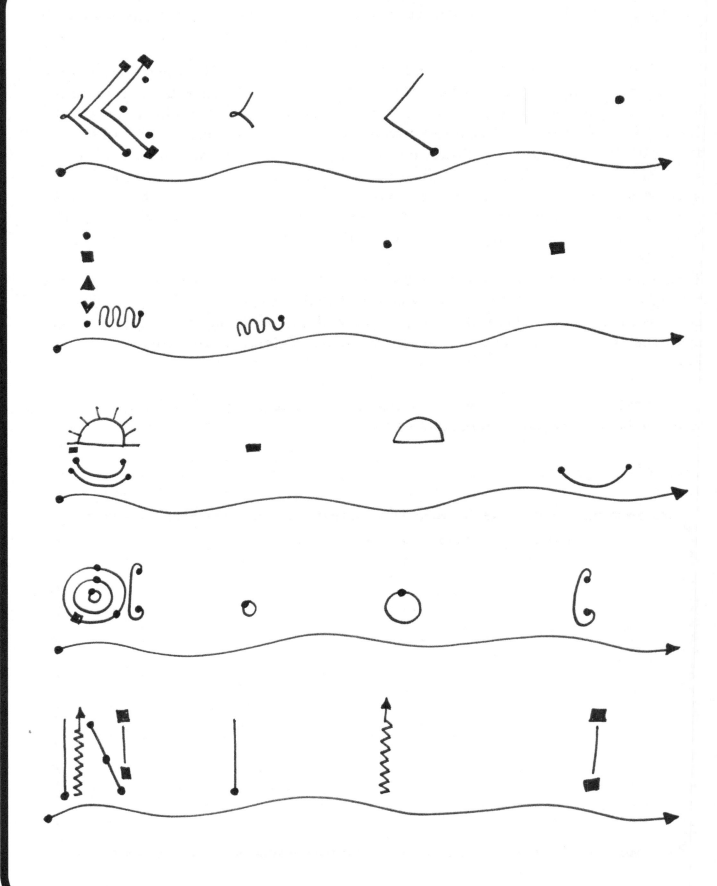

Dear New Homeschool Mom,

What a wonderful adventure you are embarking on. It will be very different than anything you have experienced before in education for your children. You will discover such delight and freedom. You will soon see that you learn just as much as your children. The greatest thing is that you will have such a great bond in the family, and you will have a whole new way of life. True learning comes by interest, support, experiences, and exploration. Remember, you care the most about your child and know what they need. You cannot fail in home schooling because it's rooted in love and love never fails!

You are equipping your children to become clever & successful individuals. There is no greater reward in life!

Blessings in your journey,
Krista Walkley, Homeschool GranMamma

NOTES, DOODLES, IDEAS AND TASKS:

Dear new homeschooler,

Welcome! You've made a tough decision, and you can do this! It's an amazing new world and it will be filled with many ups and downs. Watch your child(ren) and see what makes them light up. Set the example that learning isn't what happens at school, but rather is what we do our entire lives! Know that whatever you are feeling, someone else has been there, too. Find them and learn from them! Welcome again to a great adventure!

Janet Salut

NOTES, DOODLES, IDEAS AND TASKS:

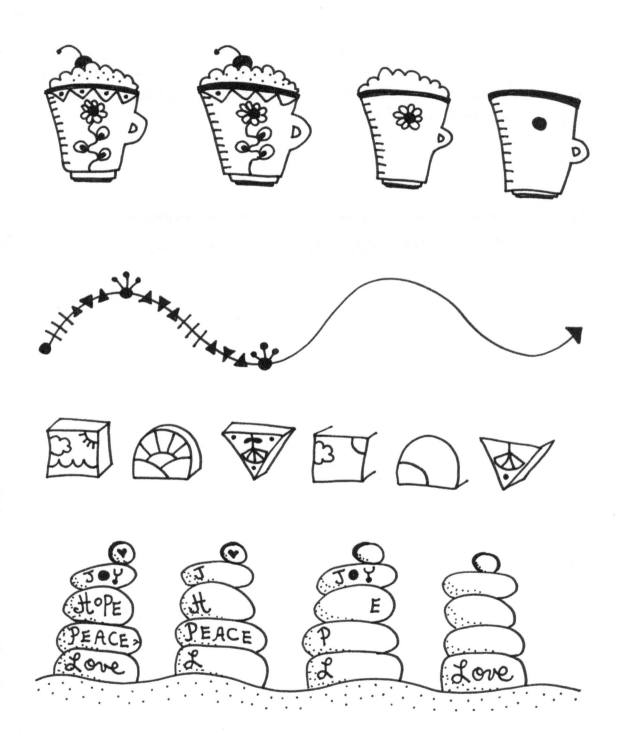

Dear new homeschooling mama,

First, welcome to the club. In this club we do days full of sunshine and rainbows, days that become a stage show for miraculous moments, days where that tough thing "clicks" for the first time and light illuminates previously dark places, days where you feel like everything and everyone have fallen into their respective places to grow and thrive together. But do you know what else we do? We do a lot of real life, nitty gritty, full steam ahead, live and in action hot mess express with a side of struggle bus, that includes spilled coffee, diaper blow outs, mysterious sticky substances on the dining room table, and a side of tears for everyone... mom included. And the best part is... learning happens on both of those kinds of days!! Your kids will learn on your best and your worst day, you have not been called to this adventure because you will do it perfectly, in fact, quite the opposite... you've been called to this choice to learn alongside your children.

You've been called to provide exactly what you have to offer everyday- yourself. Learning is a science of relationships you lay out all the things on the table like a feast before them. Math, reading, grammar, science, poetry, art, baking, sports, music, writing, anything else they love. Then you invite them in to form the relationship with all the beautiful things the world has to offer. Bite by bite they will surprise you with how they can grow to know and experience this world and all the glorious things there are to learn in their own way, in their own time.

No matter how hard you try, no matter how rigorous a schedule you try to set no two days will look the same. Embrace the chaos alongside the days that go exactly as you'd hoped and know that this is a process where small efforts (when watered over time) are honored with great rewards. When you jump in with both feet trusting that it is going to be okay, and that your children will be okay too. I promise their education will exceed all you have intended or imagined! You've got this, mama!

P.S. Don't compare yourself to any "perfect moms" on Instagram or Pinterest. Comparison is the thief of joy and for everything that she does well there is something in her homeschool that she desperately wishes she did "better" too.

All My Love,
Megan Boman

Dear Mama,

      You are enough. You have everything you need to be your child's best teacher.
Breathe and trust yourself. It will be hard. It will be fun. It will push you to your limits. You will learn so many things about your kids. Don't rush or push or stress. Do read books, play games, and laugh. Don't keep doing something that isn't working. Do pay attention to what is working and do more of that. Don't keep going through tears and frustration. Do gives lots of snuggles, snacks, and breaks. Remember that there is no perfect curriculum or method and trust yourself to know what is best for your child. You've got this.

Jenny Hedrick

NOTES, DOODLES, IDEAS AND TASKS:

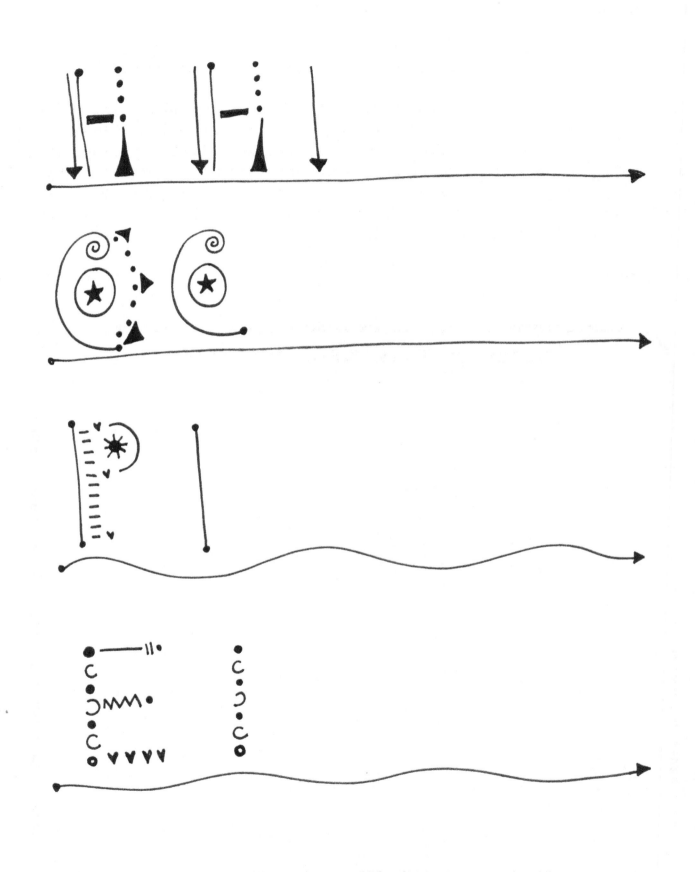

Dear new homeschool mom,

Look at you, taking a stand for what you believe is best for your babies! We moms will do anything for our kids. Remember that. You will need this reminder throughout your journey. Now, congratulations on making this amazing decision to empower your children through home education! You're about to do so much more than you thought. Just wait and see. I know it seems scary. Maybe you feel overwhelmed and nervous. Perhaps a little crazy, but you're not! Sometimes stepping away from the norm can make us doubt ourselves, but you must stand firm in your decision. No one knows your child like you. Your relationship alone will be a beacon of light when self-doubt creeps in. Just trust yourself, have confidence in your decision, and enjoy watching your kids grow into who they are meant to be. You are teaching them so much more than you even know!

Love,
Krystal Andersen- fellow homeschool mom

NOTES, DOODLES, IDEAS AND TASKS:

Dear brave parent,

Congratulations on your new adventure! Dive right in, not with books or sharpened pencils, but with time together. Read, explore, go on field trips, go for hikes, ask your children what they want to learn, play, or read. Time is so fleeting, enjoy the gift of being their teacher. It is a heavy responsibility while at the same time a fulfilling and joyful journey. Remember, you have always taught them...to talk, to walk, to use a potty, so many things. Homeschool is an extension of all the parenting you've already been doing. Trust that you know them better than anyone. Watch how they learn and what they soak up, where they seek more. Learn alongside them and enjoy. Find a tribe, fellow homeschoolers are an amazing resource and support! Some days you will need an extra cup of coffee or tea to keep going. Some days you'll need to drop everything and all go on a walk to reset the day. Some days skipping rocks will count as science. Some days will have tears, good or bad, and some days will have so much laughter. Remember this is a journey not a destination. Blessings over you and all the little minds you help expand and grow.

Jessica Terpstra, Veteran Homeschool Mom

NOTES, DOODLES, IDEAS AND TASKS:

Dear new homeschool mom,

What a brave decision you have made! I know it won't always be easy, but it'll be so worth it! And I am excited for your new adventure with your children! It's not an adventure you are likely to forget either. Take it moment by moment and day by day. Don't stress over what others think your homeschooling day should look like and remember that each child learns differently, and each mama teaches differently. So just don't compare your journey with anyone else's! Remember that sometimes school is learning to make a new recipe, snuggling up on the couch with a new book and reading aloud together, or hiking in the woods. School doesn't have to be the traditional "book" work. It can be so much more! It can be joyful! It can be a learning feast! Find the school that brings you joy and leave the stressful behind! Enjoy your adventure and be blessed in your journey!

Sarah Skelton

NOTES, DOODLES, IDEAS AND TASKS:

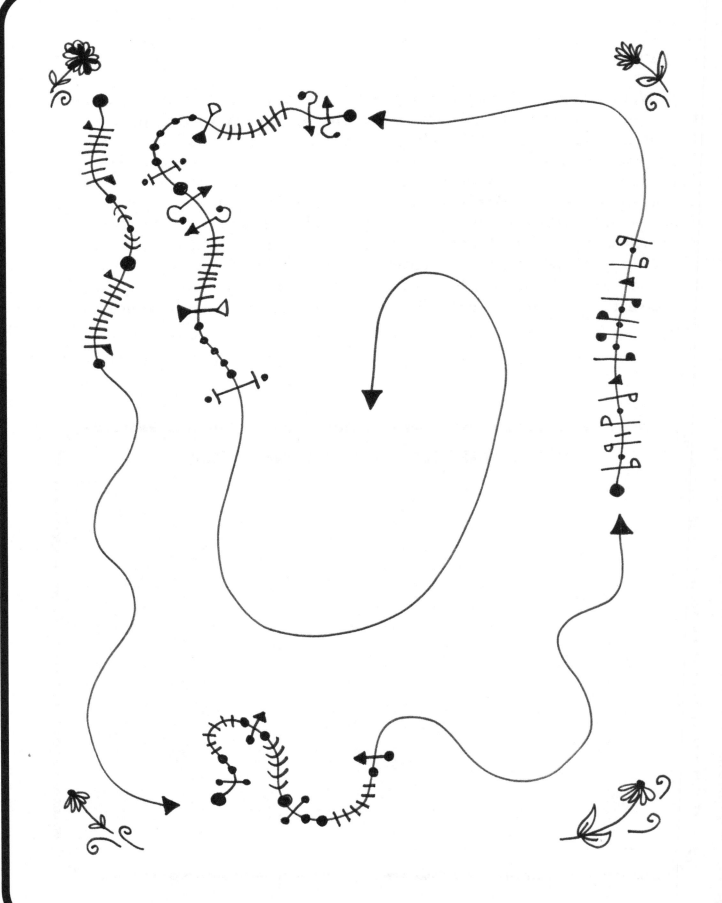

Dear new homeschool mama,

Welcome to the adventure because that is what this is, a wonderfully fun, glorious adventure. Remember that this is your adventure with your child. You may be new to homeschooling, but your children are new to life. They will learn how to love learning from your love of learning. Find it in yourself first and embrace it. Remember all the things you wanted to do as a kid that you couldn't because of school or other things? Do them now with your kids. Go to the beach, run in the woods, build things, sew, knit, draw, paint, travel if you can, make life and adventure for them and yourself. They will learn "all the things" they need to, but more importantly they will learn to love learning and be lifelong learners and so will you.

One last thing. If you ever feel yourselves backsliding, losing your joy in homeschooling, take time to stop and reevaluate. Reset and regroup. Remember what made the adventure an adventure and start doing that again. Things will not always be perfect, but you will always be building on the good memories you make. Onward new homeschooling mom, onward!

NOTES, DOODLES, IDEAS AND TASKS:

New Homescchooling Mom,

So this is your first year homeschooling, Congratulations on the first step to freedom and the love to learn. Your journey will be filled with ups and downs and of course the fear of missing out. Don't worry, everyone is different and learn at different rates. Just take a deep breath and remember this is about you as much as it is about your child. If you're happy they will be too.

Be open to the possibilities of learning new skills following a path that isn't considered normal or traditional. I would encourage you to be part of the Fun-Schooling Community! This group is amazing and I hope you feel welcomed and accepted. Feel free to ask questions, us moms need to stick together and are always happy to help.

With Love,

Yesenia Gonzalez

NOTES, DOODLES, IDEAS AND TASKS:

Dear brave, new- homeschool mama,

You were made for this! The Lord so graciously blessed you with a child or many children to raise. It is no mistake you are stumbling upon this letter. Please, take to heart these words and let your brain let go of the worldly ways. You have many, many gifts to offer your blessing and it is such a gift and sanctification work to share those with your offspring. The enemy will try to push you to self-doubt, but God- already prepared the steps and the way, all you must do is step into that path. It's a daily happiness and joy to get to do life with the little people you call family and no matter how hard the moments can be, He can use them for His glory. Give yourself and your child the Grace that HE so lovingly bestows upon you in the learning process. The daily tasks can seem daunting, but if you look through the lens of love and grace- your perspective will change. You were made for such a time as this! Go for it, mama!!

Love,
Haley Cole, mom of twins plus a few more arrows

NOTES, DOODLES, IDEAS AND TASKS:

Dear new homeschooling mom,

I am so excited for you and your family, as this decision will bring years of precious memories for you all. Please do not fall into the trap of trying to be perfect or Pinterest worthy or recreate the school system in your home. You are so much more than that! You are the person the Father entrusted those children to and so are perfectly equipped to give them the exactly unique education He would have for them. It is His standard by which we are accountable and not the man made constructs the world would have us force our children into. You are the perfect fit for this role and the Creator of the Universe already approved you for the position.

So enjoy this time! Relish in every little moment of discovery. Every light bulb moment. You get to be your child's witness to all they delight in as you learn together. What a privilege you have!!!

In Him,

Jenny Kusch

NOTES, DOODLES, IDEAS AND TASKS:

Dear Struggling Mom,

A mom asked the question, *"How do you deal with mom guilt? The feeling that it's just never enough, and you're never enough and can never be good enough or do good enough?"*

Let me tell you why you are so afraid of getting it wrong. You were probably educated under a system that searched for your mistakes, and you were constantly being judged by what you did wrong. You would complete your work, and your teacher would take it and grade it. And how are papers usually graded? By finding all the mistakes and pointing them all out to the child. That's very likely what we grew up with. So now we have become adults, and we've become parents and homeschool moms who are still afraid of making mistakes.

Please don't raise kids who are afraid of making mistakes. Mistakes are normal. It's through making mistakes and trying things that we learn how to overcome, and we learn to be okay with not being perfect. We learn about trying again. You are not the sum of your mistakes and your imperfections.

Let me give you an example about how to change your perspective. If you're a mom who grades her child's papers, here's what you need to do. Let's say your child did a creative writing project. And they fill an entire page with a story. The traditional educator in you is going to look at their creative writing and you are going to put a line under every mistake. Then you'll tell the child that they spelled **20** words wrong.

Here's what the Fun-Schooling mom will do: You will look at the creative writing page, and you will circle every single thing they did right. Then you are going to say, "Wow, you just wrote a **400**-word paper, and you got **350** words correct!"

That is so much more encouraging than saying, "You got **50** things wrong."

Focus on what they did right, especially if it is a creative project. If your child is being creative, focus on the story, on the heart, and on character. Stop focusing on their mistakes. We are ruining kids by obsessing over mistakes and judging them by everything they are doing wrong instead of what they are doing right. Of course, kids are going to make mistakes.

Kids will learn best when they are motivated by their passions, hobbies, joys, collaborating, exploring, bonding and smiles. The joy of learning is lost when school revolves around the child's failures instead of their little victories. The joy of being a homeschooling mom is lost when perfectionism takes over. Be you. Be imperfect. Be fun. Be relaxed. Be a mom, not a school master. Enjoy progress and togetherness and don't forget to experiment, play and put relationship first.

Blessings,

Sarah Janisse Brown

NOTES, DOODLES, IDEAS AND TASKS:

Made in the USA
Coppell, TX
05 February 2023

12153299R10050